Journey to Gameland

Journey to Gameland

*How to Make a Board Game
from Your Favorite Children's Book*

Ben Buchanan, Carol J. Adams
and Susan Kay Allison

Illustrated by Doug Buchanan

LANTERN BOOKS

NEW YORK

2001
Lantern Books
One Union Square West, Suite 201
New York, NY 10003

Printed in the United States of America

Library of Congress Cataloguing-in-Publication Data

Buchanan, Ben.
Journey to Gameland : how to make a board game from your
favorite children's book / Ben Buchanan, Carol J. Adams, and Susan Allison ;
illustrated by Doug Buchanan.
p. cm.
Includes bibliographical references.
ISBN 1-930051-51-4 (alk. paper)
1. Board games—Design and construction—Juvenile literature.
2. Gameboards—Design and construction—Juvenile literature.
3. Children's literature. [1. Board games. 2. Games. 3. Books and reading.]
I. Adams, Carol J. II. Allison, Susan, 1958-III.
Buchanan, Doug, ill. IV. Title.

GV1312 .B83 2001
794—DC21
2001029464

to our parents and teachers
and all adults who share the joy of
reading with children

Contents

INVITATION TO GAMELAND

ear Reader,

You are invited to a very special place.

Some kids think this world is all there is. When they are frustrated about their favorite television program being cancelled, they kick in the TV. Can you think of someone like that?

But other kids know there is an entire other world.... A world where magic happens! A world they can go to whenever they want.

Where is this world?

Oz? Hogwarts? Middle Earth? Wonderland? Redwall?

No. It's your mind!

It is your imagination—especially when you are inspired by a good book.

The following pages will show you how to use your own creativity to enjoy your favorite books even more. They will tell you how to make your very own game based on the characters and places of your favorite book. One child, Ben, has already done this, and he tells his story in a companion volume, *My Year with Harry Potter.*

You can have so much fun making your own game! Ben's mom, Carol, and the children's librarian from Ben's local public library, Susan, have helped Ben put this book together so that you can take your very own creative journey.

Continued on page 10

For this journey, you will need some materials, such as scissors, paper, and glue. (See page 19 for the list of "What to Pack.") Just as with many trips, you will fill out postcards. This time, they are here to help you in your planning process for creating your own game. Yes, you can write in this book! Write whatever you want, because it is your journey. And you don't have to do this alone. We know kids who sat down and together created a game. They had lots of fun. Or you can have a party. In the pages that follow, we tell you how to have a "Make Your Own Board Game" Party, too.

"Ben suggests" are little stories from Ben about how he created his game. At the end of the book is a Master of Gameland Certificate. Congratulations! It is for you! Celebrate what you have accomplished by making your own board game!

Adults want to be a part of the magic of the books you love, too. That is because they may have loved them when they were children or discovered their marvels as adults. Your favorite books are important to them, so we have included a letter to the adults in your life, and throughout the book we have little "guideposts" to provide information for grown ups about your trip. But this is *your* book, and it is *your* journey.

You bring the most important ingredient to this journey. What is that? Enthusiasm for your favorite book? Well that goes without saying. But you bring something even more important than that—your own creativity. Enjoy every step of your way.

Let's begin our journey!

Ben, Carol, Susan

Teachers, Parents, Librarians, and other Travel Agents

Some of the best trips in childhood are taken through the pages of a beloved book. We get to visit and live with—for a short while—favorite characters, who remain with us through our lives. You know which books are cherished by children. You have read them to the children in your life. Perhaps you have shared a favorite book from your childhood, like *The Wizard of Oz* or *Alice in Wonderland*. Or perhaps together with your children you have discovered the joy of Harry Potter.

Kids all over the world have fallen in love with reading thanks to the magic of J. K. Rowling. Many readers have read her books multiple times in order to prolong the magic they cast over their readers, who are reluctant to leave the books' mystical landscape. You may have read the books along with your children, and be as thrilled as they are when a new one comes out. Classic children's books can fascinate the entire family with their magic. But how can you extend the magic of the favorite books that draw children into reading?

A very special young man recently discovered a way to extend the magic of J. K. Rowling while waiting with millions of other kids for Book IV to be released. His name is Ben Buchanan and he created his own Harry Potter game—a board game based on the Harry Potter series. Ben describes creating his own game in a companion volume, *My Year with Harry Potter.* I, Susan, a children's librarian and former elementary school teacher, found it refreshing to know that, in today's world of commercial board and video games, a child can find enjoyment and satisfaction in the creation and playing of his own game. Ben even shared the game with about 100 children of different ages by collaborating in a program at our local public library. It was amazing to observe so many kids sharing a reading experience together as they debated various points in the books and created games together. All the energy that evolved from the sharing of a children's book was truly inspirational.

Your child can experience this magic of creating a board game based on their favorite book with a little help and encouragement from you, the aid of materials you have around the house, and the imagination and creativity that all youngsters possess.

The authors of this book believe that children should be treated as creators not as consumers. In the spirit of that understanding, we have taken the experience of one child, and used it as the backdrop against which any child can discover and develop their creative skills.

This is a child-friendly activity, encouraging and empowering children. Each child can enter into the spirit of creativity that every classic children's book captures. Each adult who helps a child create a game gets to help the child think imaginatively. But that is not all. This is a family-friendly activity, too. After all, when the game is done, who better to play it than the family?!

In the following pages, you and your child will learn the steps Ben went through to create his game, and the ways that you can help your child. Your family will learn together that creating a board game based on a great book in children's literature will result in more than just fun—it will exercise your child's verbal comprehension, their math talents, and their sequencing, analyzing, synthesizing, and organizing skills. After all, think about what a game requires: it needs rules and playing pieces, obstacles, and some way of measuring progress and defeat. As your child decides the rules of their game, how it will be structured and what difficulties it will present, various intellectual and mental skills are being developed.

Whenever we take a trip, we adults often want our kids to stop and appreciate the historical markers along the way. They are hanging out the window while we say, "Look, this was built in the seventeenth century." Clearly, we often have different travel expectations than our kids do for the same experience. Each of the tasks that your child can follow to create his or her own game, is, in fact, educational and strengthens various academic skills. In the pages that follow, we provide not "historical markers" but "guideposts" to identify for adults the strengths the child derives from the different activities in game creation. We have also identified ways that your children can create this game without too much adult supervision (or interference!). You might gather together the materials and let them proceed at their own pace.

Often we forget how much a kind word and loving attention can do for any of us. Children, especially, thrive on positive words and feelings. When your child shows an interest in doing the projects in the book, praise them for their interest, and for all of their efforts. Be enthusiastic about everything they accomplish, no matter how small.

Encourage your child to take the risk of creating something themselves. You can say, "I know it seems harder to create your own, but you can do it."

I, Carol, Ben's mom, was at times tempted to get more involved in his project. It was time-consuming! It was complex! It required patience on his part, and on mine. But Ben would say, "Let me do it." Or "I can figure it out." Even if your child isn't that assertive, assume them to be so, and give them the space to create. This sort of space isn't so much a place (though a table to work on is helpful!), as a sense of possibility. It was wonderful to see how much Ben loved his favorite book, and to watch him extend it through creating his game. The game became a way to keep the magic of the book alive and fresh. It also became very exciting for me to see what Ben could develop, and then to be available to help him in the very few places where help was required (usually typing).

Susan Cooper, a wise writer, has said, "The truth is that *every* book we read, like every person we meet, has the capacity to change our lives.

And though we can be sure our children will meet people, we must, must create, these days, their chance to meet books."[*] What better way to meet a great book than to design a game based upon it! In doing so, your child is given the greatest gift of all—an encounter with his or her own creativity. Yes, they will be able to enjoy their favorite book in yet another way. And that is thrilling in and of itself. But, in manipulating the story and looking at it in new, and creative, ways your child encounters not just the world of a fictional character, but their own abilities. Through creating a game, they meet themselves.

A *Journey to Gameland* is a special and unforgettable experience for all involved—enjoy the trip!

Signed,

Carol, Susan

[*] Barbara Elleman, *Books Change Lives: Quotes to Treasure*. Chicago: American Library Association, 1994, no pagination.

GUIDEPOST

Tips for Grown Ups

Read the book(s) together. If you need ideas for good books, look at the list at the back of the book or ask your librarian. Librarians love to give you great books to read!

Talk about the book with your children.

Before you start, consider the age of your children. Will the children be able to do most of the work independently or will they require your assistance with a few aspects of it? For children to be able to independently create their own board game, we believe they probably need to be in third grade or higher.

How much should you help? Encourage them all you can! Support them, praise them, and talk with them.

Encourage creative thinking. Try not to discourage your child by responding "I don't think that will work." Talk ideas through with your child and let them discover conclusions and results on their own.

Listen to your child. If they are having a problem envisioning something or building something, don't help them solve it immediately. Hear them as they describe the problem. Help them brainstorm. A *hands-on* activity for them is often a *hands-off* activity for us.

Throughout this book you will find suggestions for research possibilities for your child at the local library. Think of these "detours" as Library Scavenger Hunts. Don't answer your children's questions, but help them discover the joy of researching the answers for themselves. Your children's librarian will be glad to help.

We have tried to anticipate those areas where a child might encounter difficulties or become frustrated. These are labeled, "Roadblocks." Let your child know that everyone encounters problems in a creative project and that it is normal not to get things right the first time. *(Continued on next page)*

GUIDEPOST

(Continued from previous page)

Show an interest in what your child is doing, but don't compare your child's creation to Ben's or anyone else's. It is theirs, and that makes it beautiful and significant. Focus on the strengths of what they have done—through their own creativity, they have made a book world three-dimensional.

CHAPTER 1

Before You Go:
How to Use this Book

This book has several parts to it. What are they?

POSTCARDS

Just as you might send postcards to friends and family when you are traveling to tell them about your
journey, we have included "postcards." But these
postcards are different. You write them to and for

yourself. They are provided to help you narrow down the possibilities
for your game by helping you organize your thoughts about your
favorite book.

SOUVENIRS

Once you know what you want to create for your board game,
the "souvenirs" sections provide directions for things you
can create. They are activities for you to follow if you
wish.

DETOURS

As you think about your favorite book, and the parts that you really love, you may discover that there are some parts or references that you don't really understand. What should you do? Go to your local library and ask your librarian to help you research! You may discover an exciting aspect to the book that you simply must include in your game. Detours are Knowledge Scavenger Hunts! Have fun.

GUIDEPOSTS

Guideposts provide direction. Adults often are the guide-posts of our lives. The guideposts in this book help to identify for adults the strengths that you are gaining from the different activities in game creation.

BEN SUGGESTS

Along your path, Ben will offer suggestions based on his experience creating his Harry Potter Game.

ROADBLOCKS

Stuck? That's OK. Roadblocks happen on trips. Roadblocks make you slow down and rethink the direction you're going in. Everybody runs into roadblocks along the way—so pause, think, and re-consider.

C H A P T E R 2

What to Pack

Here is a list of materials you could use. You won't need everything on the list. But this is to spark your imagination. You can see how things around the house can be used for your game.

- Cardboard/posterboard

- File folders (you can use either letter size or legal size)

- Candies in various shapes for creating game pieces, like wands

- Toothpicks

- Construction paper

- Scissors

- Glue or Tape

- Brads

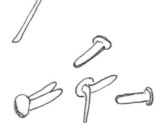

- Markers or crayons

- Pencil

- Envelope, small box, or other container to hold game

- Gold/silver wrapping paper or aluminum foil for money

- Three-by-five-inch index cards

- Flour, salt, and food coloring

- Paints

- Sticky notes

CHAPTER 3

Planning Your Trip

Before you go on a trip, you have to decide where you want to go. To create your own board game, ask yourself: What is my very favorite book? Maybe your answer is that you have lots of favorite books.

[POSTCARD]

List your favorite books:

- _____

- _____

- _____

- _____

- _____

- _____

Here are some questions you can ask yourself about these books:

Which book have I read more than once? _____

_____

Which book have I asked someone else to read to me more than once?

_____

Which book have I recommended to a friend? _____

_____

Which book have I discussed with a friend? _____

_____

Which book has my favorite character in it? _____

_____

Which book has a special place on my bookshelf? _____

_____

Look at your list. Does one book appear as the answer to several of these questions? If the answer is yes, that is probably your favorite book.

BEN

SUGGESTS

Of course, Harry Potter was my first thought because it was my favorite book. But, if I hadn't read Harry Potter there would have been others to choose from. And it would have been a hard choice. Would I want to use Lewis Carroll's *Alice in Wonderland*, or Philip Pullman's *The Golden Compass*, or maybe Daniel Pinkwater's *Alan Mendelsohn: The Boy from Mars*?

If, like Ben, you were to discover that more than one book comes to mind as a favorite book, you can ask yourself some questions based on the type of book you might want to base your game around:

Would you like to do a mystery game? What is your favorite mystery book? _____

Would you like your game set on another planet? What is your favorite science fiction book? _____

Would you like your game to be an adventure? What is your favorite adventure or historical fiction book? _____

Would you like your game to be set in an imaginary place? What is your favorite fantasy book? _____

What an exciting variety of books there are! At this point, one book probably stands out as your favorite. What book are you going to base your board game on? _____

Are you lost and don't know where to go? Go to the Appendix on pp. 97–101 for some ideas from our librarian for books and themes to get you started.

CHAPTER 4

Following Your Mind's Journey

When we are reading, our mind goes on a journey. We are taken to fabulous places and it is natural to want to bring souvenirs back from these places. Journeying through a book isn't like walking on the beach, where we can bend down and select our favorite shells or rocks. But, just as you pick up souvenirs to remember your trip, you can collect words, phrases, and ideas off the pages of your favorite book. You can recapture what you have read and loved by writing down ideas and thoughts.

You already know what your favorite book is. Why not take some three-by-five-inch cards or a blank piece of paper for a bookmark, and start reading again? Notice: Does your mind start to think of ideas for your game? When you read about Pippi Longstocking's pancakes, do you imagine a kitchen in your board game? Or, when you read about Alice in Wonderland, do you start imagining the garden? Or, when you pick up your favorite volume of Harry Potter, do you discover your mind starts to imagine Hogwarts' halls? That is your mind taking a journey. The journey is sparked by the book, but its direction is guided by your imagination.

{ POSTCARD }

Pick your favorite chapter in your favorite book. As you read it, stop and write down what you are enjoying. What have you noticed?

Have you noticed things in the book that make you smile or laugh?

Have you noticed things that happen between the characters that excite you because they involve courage or cooperation or disagreement?

Have you noticed the way the author describes someone or somewhere?

Write about what you have noticed here:

_____

_____

_____

_____

_____

_____

_____

_____

_____

_____

_____

When people go on trips they often keep a travel journal so they can remember the details of their trip when they get home. You are doing the same thing, getting ready to create your board game based on what you love in your favorite book.

Two important parts of following your mind's journey are: writing down your ideas and keeping track of the ideas you have written down! You should do this the way that is best for you.

★ Some kids like to keep journals. If you are one of those, start a special journal for your favorite book. Write in the journal whenever you have an idea or a response to your book. If you notice that you have dreams about your favorite book, write them down in your journal, too.

★ Some kids don't want to write in a journal. If you want to keep your ideas on three-by-five-inch cards, create an "idea box." This is a box that will hold the three-by-five-inch cards you have written on until you are ready to start working on your board game.

★ Keep a blank piece of paper in your favorite book as your bookmark and write down your thoughts on that.

BEN

SUGGESTS

At first I didn't want to write down an idea when I had it, especially when I was in the car. I would say to my mom, "I'll remember it." But she always had me write it down, even though we might have been bumping along the road. I am glad I did! When I went to create the spaces on the board, I had a list of ideas already!

CHAPTER 5

Consulting a Map: Determining the Beginning and End of Your Game

Like all trips and all good books, your game needs a beginning and an ending. But it may not be exactly the same beginning or ending that your favorite book has. For instance, if you are creating a game based on *The Wonderful Wizard of Oz* you might decide that it should focus on getting Dorothy to Emerald City. You might begin in Munchkinland and end when Dorothy is knocking on the door to Emerald City. You might select this section of the book because it was the most exciting section, because Dorothy made new friends there, and because you have a sense of her achieving one of her goals.

BEN

SUGGESTS

For my Harry Potter game, I asked myself "What part of the book (*Harry Potter and the Sorcerer's Stone*) did you like the most?" This is how my answers looked:

What I liked the most is when they go through the trap door.
Why?
Because it was exciting.
What made it so exciting?
Everything they had to do to get through the obstacles.
So I decided to make a game out of the trap door or put trap doors into my game.

What part of your favorite book did you like the most? Fill out the postcard and discover what really interests you.

POST CARD

{ P O S T C A R D }

What book have you chosen? _____

What part of the book did you like the most? _____

_____

_____

_____

Why did you like that part? Answer: I liked that part because

_____

_____

Look at your answer. You said you liked it because it was

_____

_____

What made it so ? _____

_____

What you are doing is choosing the actions that take place in the favorite part of your book. List these actions in the order in which they happen:

1. _____

2. _____

3. _____

4. _____

5. _____

6. _____

7. _____

8. _____

Now see if you can imagine them as squares on a board game.

★ Could the first action be at the beginning of your game?

★ Can the problems that arise be squares in your game?

★ Do you like the way that part of the book ends? Can you see it being the goal for your game?

These questions are helping you to decide what direction your board game will go in. They will help you as you develop the squares for your game in the following chapters.

GUIDEPOST

Analysis: Your child is using what she or he comprehended from a favorite book, exhibiting a broad understanding of the plot, characters, and action. He or she is analyzing what worked and choosing details they enjoyed the most. At this stage, they are learning to go from the big picture to specific details, showing an understanding of narrowing the main idea.

CHAPTER 6

Destination. Where Are You Going? Choosing the Object of Your Board Game

The object of the game identifies *how you win*. Think about the kinds of board games you have played. Some games end because someone won points or money. Some end because a destination was reached. Some combine both.

Imagine you choose *Alice in Wonderland* as your favorite book. You decide that you want Alice to have to get somewhere (a destination has to be reached) and also that she will need to have a certain amount of money when she gets there (money has to be gotten). You might say that the *object of my game* is that Alice is lost and she needs to get to a phone booth with enough money to call home.

My game will begin at Alice falling into Wonderland.

My game will end at Alice reaching the phone booth with enough money to call home.

BEN
SUGGESTS

Did you notice something in our last answer? There is no phone booth in *Alice in Wonderland*, is there? Don't let that stop you! It is your game. Be creative. You can take parts of the book you love and add elements to it. Or you can have characters do something that is not in the book. That is what I did with my game, Harry Potter and the Search for the Lost Treasure. Searching for lost treasure doesn't happen in any of the books, but I liked the idea of it, and it tied in with my favorite game, Monopoly™. The idea gave me the freedom to imagine Harry Potter having other adventures.

Now it is your turn: How will you know who has won your game or that the game is over? The next postcards can help you answer that question.

Below are three different postcards. Read them and choose which one you like.

{ POSTCARD }

A game where winning is decided by points or money.

Do you want points or money in your game? _____

Will the person with the *most* points or money win, or must the winner have acquired a *certain* amount?

I want the winner to have_____

_____

Some things I might want to use for money are: play money, pretend coins, toothpicks, or _____

_____

31

{ POSTCARD }

A game where winning is decided by having certain tasks to complete.

Will there be tasks that have to be done? _____

Will the person who gets all the tasks done first win the game?

_____

Some things that the players might have to *do* based on what happens in my favorite book are:

★ _____

★ _____

★ _____

★ _____

★ _____

★ _____

★ _____

Some things the players might have to *get* are:

★ _____

★ _____

★ _____

★ _____

★ _____

★ _____

★ _____

─┤ POSTCARD ├─

A game where winning is decided by reaching a destination.

Will the game end because someone reaches a destination first?

_____

_____

What are some possible destinations for your game?

_____

_____

_____

_____

_____

_____

_____

_____

It is possible to have several challenges for your players. They may need to have money or points as well as tasks to do or things to get. (See Chapter 12: The Hazards of Traveling about having several challenges). But it is important, first, to have one goal. Circle the goal that you picked:

POINTS OR MONEY   TASKS   DESTINATION

That is the *object* of your game.

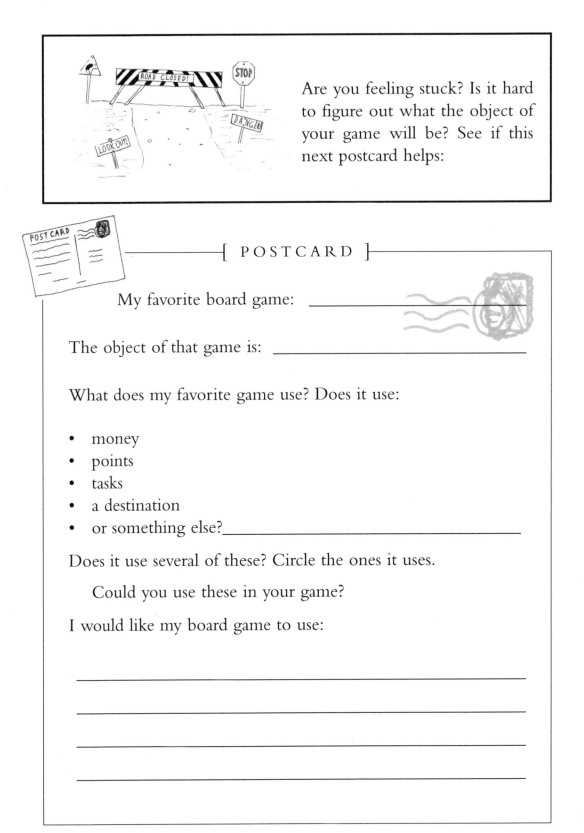

Are you feeling stuck? Is it hard to figure out what the object of your game will be? See if this next postcard helps:

{ POSTCARD }

My favorite board game: _____

The object of that game is: _____

What does my favorite game use? Does it use:

- money
- points
- tasks
- a destination
- or something else?_____

Does it use several of these? Circle the ones it uses.

Could you use these in your game?

I would like my board game to use:

_____

_____

_____

_____

Now that you have chosen what will be used as a goal of the game and how you will know who has won, you can state what the object of your game is.

The object of my game is: _____

My game will begin at_____

My game will end at _____

When you write your rules (see Chapter 15), this is where you begin, with explaining the object of your game.

GUIDEPOST

Conceptualization: With this exercise, children take the details they have pulled out of the bigger picture to conceptualize a goal or main idea. They make important connections between the book and their game. Having already decided on the beginning point, the children now know their end point. Besides helping them develop their board game, these are crucial concepts for understanding how a story is created.

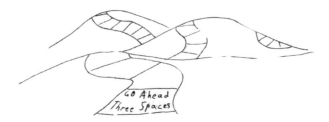

CHAPTER 7

Designing Your Route: Drawing Out Your Ideas by Creating a Board

BEN

SUGGESTS

My next step was to begin to create a board. I had to decide what the board would look like. Would it have squares to land on? Would the squares form a road, or a path? I had to figure out whether, like most board games, this path would be along the border. Would the path curve? This was a really fun and challenging part for me. I loved thinking about how to set up the board.

In this chapter you will design the shape for your board game. You don't have to worry about what will be in the squares at this point—just how your board will be shaped.

{ POSTCARD }

Think about your favorite board game. How is it shaped?

_____

Do you want to use that shape for your board game? _____

Look at the shapes Ben's brother Doug has drawn:

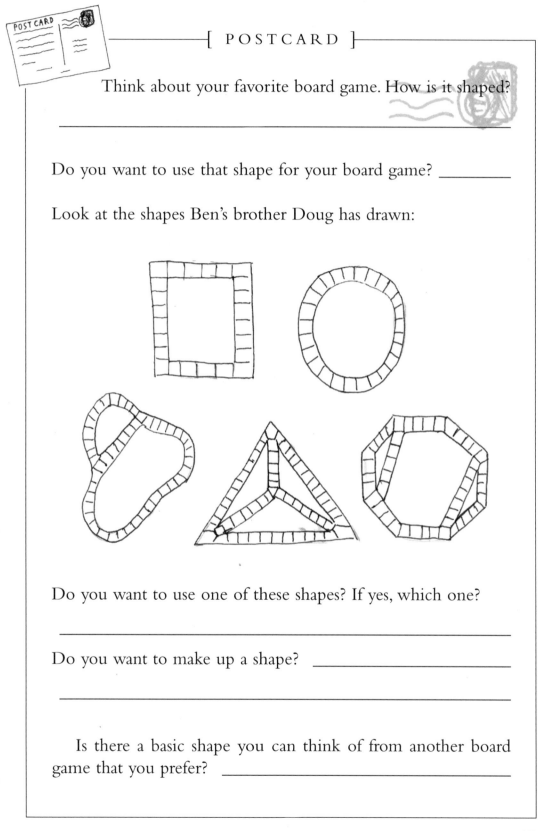

Do you want to use one of these shapes? If yes, which one?

_____

Do you want to make up a shape? _____

_____

Is there a basic shape you can think of from another board game that you prefer? _____

[POSTCARD]

Draw a design of the route of the path your players will follow in your game:

To transfer your map to a board, you need to choose what your board will be made out of. It can be a file folder. You can use cardboard.

BEN

I took boards from old games I no longer played and spray painted them.

SUGGESTS

Select your material for your board:

- Cardboard
- File Folder
- Old Board Game Board

Transfer your map onto your choice for a board. You can decorate it later, after you fill in the squares. The next chapter will guide you through this next step.

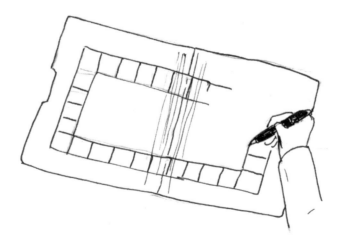

CHAPTER 8

The Scenic Route: The Details of Your Game

Sometimes we don't travel to our destination on highways. We want to get off the four lane expressways and enjoy a slow ride through the countryside. This is called "the scenic route." Here, on the scenic route, every mile of traveling is enjoyable because there is so much to see. Perhaps, your parents tell you about *points of interest*. "Over there," your father says, "is where your great great grandfather had a farm. Look at that soil! Look at the rock! How did he think he could farm there?" The landscape becomes filled with stories.

How do you fill your board game with the stories that you love from your favorite book?

BEN

SUGGESTS

That was the hardest part: Coming up with what the spaces would be. But I listened to my Harry Potter tape and that helped. And I wrote down my ideas whenever I thought of them—riding in the car was a time when I daydreamed about my board game. I was surprised by how many squares I thought of on the way to piano lessons or coming home from school.

You do it first by *naming the spaces or squares on the board.* You will name them according to the theme of your game. For instance, in Ben's game, Ben had a Hogwarts Board, so many of the spaces had to do with things that happen in Hogwarts.

Here are some suggestions for naming the spaces on your board: Think of your spaces as being places, actions, or meetings with people, animals, or other creatures.

* Your spaces can be places.
* Your spaces can be encounters with people or animals.
* Your spaces can be actions.

For instance, if you are doing a board game of *Alice in Wonderland,* you might identify as spaces:

* The White Rabbit's house (place)
* The caucus race (action)
* The table in the hole (place)
* The hole that Alice fell down (place and action)
* The caterpillar (person/animal)
* The tea party (place and action)
* The croquet game (place and action)
* The Cheshire cat (person/animal)
* The courtroom (place)

If you were making an *Alice in Wonderland* game and had selected these items for your spaces, your next step would be to assign them a place on your board. To decide where they could go, you would create a sticky note for each of these places, actions, or people/animals.

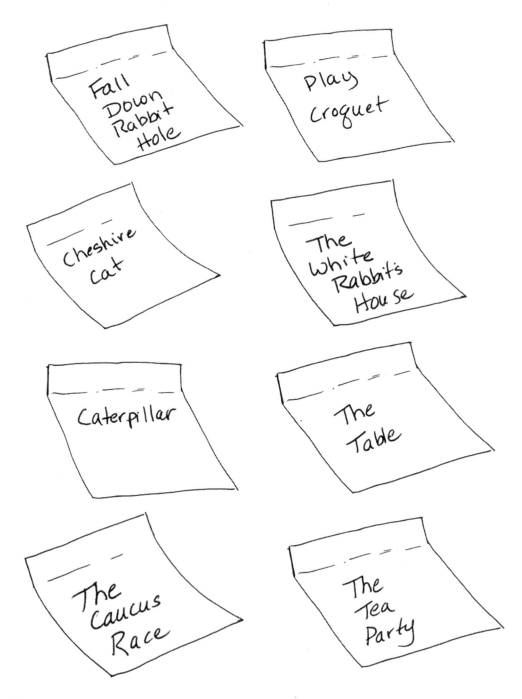

You would then place each sticky note on a space on your game board. By placing the sticky notes on your game board, you can see how the spaces are filling in. And by using sticky notes you can decide whether you want to move your spaces around or not. You might decide you want the tea party nearer the caterpillar. You also can keep track of how many spaces remain to be filled. At this point, do not fill in every space. More possibilities for spaces will be described in future chapters!

Now it is your turn to make a list of possible spaces. You have already identified many of the actions that excited you in your favorite book on p. 29. This time you will focus on people/animals and places.

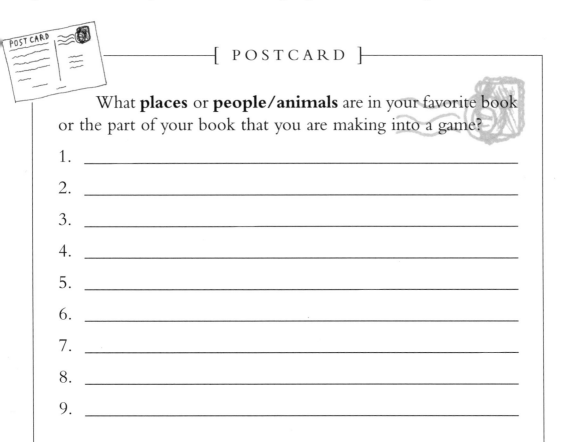

{ POSTCARD }

What **places** or **people/animals** are in your favorite book or the part of your book that you are making into a game?

1. _____
2. _____
3. _____
4. _____
5. _____
6. _____
7. _____
8. _____
9. _____

Circle at least six of them (or you can use all of them).

Write each place or person/animal on its own sticky note.
Later you might assign points or tasks to these spaces. (See Chapter 11: Tollways and Treasures and 13: Double Decker Highway.)

Are you excited by starting to fill in the spaces of your board?

If you are stuck with identifying places and people/animals, go to your library and see if there are other editions of your favorite book. By "other editions" we mean that the illustrations in the library's copy of your favorite book are different from the illustrations in your book. For instance, there are many different editions of *Alice in Wonderland* and lots of different illustrations. If there are other editions of your favorite book, look and see how different artists have depicted the places and unusual characters in your chosen book. What interesting places, creatures, and happenings show up in the illustrations?

CHAPTER 9

Who is Going?
The Characters for the Game

Now you need to decide who is going to play on your board. This may seem obvious to you. For example, if you have chosen the Harry Potter books you probably want at least Harry, Hermione, Hagrid, Ron, Malfoy, if not Professor McGonagall and Professor Dumbledore. Or if you were doing *Alice in Wonderland*, you might have Alice, the White Rabbit, the Cheshire Cat, the Doormouse, or the Mad Hatter. You can have more game pieces than players, so your players can have a choice.

Go to the library and research the history of board games. What culture is thought to have had the first board game? What sort of pieces did they use? What shapes were their boards? Could you still have fun playing their game today?

How many game pieces do you want your players to choose from? _____

Do you want humans or nonhuman characters or both?

_____

Do you want inanimate objects like broomsticks or ruby red shoes? What inanimate objects do you want to use? _____

_____

Brainstorm some things you would like as pieces:

1. _____

2. _____

3. _____

4. _____

5. _____

6. _____

7. _____

8. _____

9. _____

10. _____

Now comes an exciting part. Creating your pieces!

Think of all the possibilities for your figurines. You can make them very simple or you can spend a lot of time on them. It is all up to you. For instance, if you wish to make simple pieces, you could select some rocks and paint them different colors and they could represent different characters or objects. Or you could use different colored jelly beans, buttons, or shells.

You may want to create your own pieces so that they look like characters from your book. You might choose to have:

* Slotted paper figures
* Cardboard figures
* Origami paper figures
* Clay figures. You can purchase clay or you can make your own.

How to make a slotted paper figurine:

1. Draw the shape you want for your figurine.
2. Copy it over again. Cut each of these copies out.
3. On one shape, draw a line from the bottom to the middle.
4. On the other shape, draw a line from the top to the middle.
5. Cut each line.
6. Put the two shapes together by inserting one with the line cut in the top into one with the line cut in the bottom. See how they stand!

Make Your Own Clay

You'll Need:

- 1 cup flour (be sure it is not self-rising)
- 1/2 cup salt
- 1/2 cup water
- 1/2 teaspoon vegetable oil
- food coloring or paint

What to Do:

Combine flour, salt, about half of the water, and all of the oil. You want your dough to be like pie dough—not too sticky or wet, but not dry and crumbly. Using your hands, mix the dough until it is smooth. If the dough isn't holding together, slowly add in more water.

You can paint your figurines or use colored clay.

If you are going to *paint your characters*, begin to shape the dough into your different characters. To connect different parts of the clay, brush a little water on them, so that these parts will stick together. (You don't want an arm to fall off when your character is reaching for something important!) They will dry overnight and then you can paint them.

OR

If instead of painting the characters, you want to have the dough be different colors, divide the dough into portions. Think about what color you will need your characters to be. Use food coloring to make the color dough you need. Mix it in well. Then create your characters, being sure to use water as glue to hold the parts together.

This recipe will make one-and-a-half cups of clay. Store it in a container with a tight lid. This recipe will keep for several months.

Game pieces can be based on animals from your book. And they can be made with paper! Origami teaches you how to make animal shapes out of paper. Here is one example:

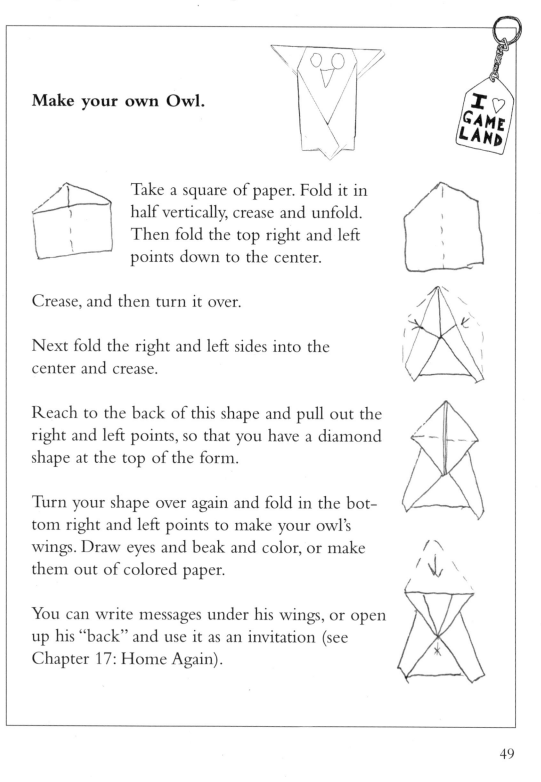

Make your own Owl.

Take a square of paper. Fold it in half vertically, crease and unfold. Then fold the top right and left points down to the center.

Crease, and then turn it over.

Next fold the right and left sides into the center and crease.

Reach to the back of this shape and pull out the right and left points, so that you have a diamond shape at the top of the form.

Turn your shape over again and fold in the bottom right and left points to make your owl's wings. Draw eyes and beak and color, or make them out of colored paper.

You can write messages under his wings, or open up his "back" and use it as an invitation (see Chapter 17: Home Again).

Do you like paper folding? Your library probably has many books about origami and making things with paper. Go to your library and find the crafts section and explore new ways to make things to go with your game.

BEN SUGGESTS

Make your own broomstick! This is what I did: I took three toothpicks. I cut off the pointy tips and then I glued them together. I cut yellow construction paper into strips. Then I cut the strips almost all the way through. Finally I wrapped the strips around the tooth-picks to make a broomstick.

GUIDEPOST

Making connections: A fun part of designing a board game is the addition of details—embellishments that enrich the playing experience. In creating these, a child will be drawing upon his or her understanding of specific details the author includes, and using them to make broader connections to their game. They will find at this point that they are looking at the book in a new way, and developing a greater understanding of the elements, by manipulating them in a new, creative way.

CHAPTER 10

How Do We Travel?
How Are You Going to Move
Along the Board?

Look at the board games you already play. How do characters move? Usually, it is through dice or spinners. How do you want your game pieces to be moved? Of course, you can use dice or spinners. But, you can also make special dice or a special spinner that draws upon what happens in your favorite book. This chapter will teach you how to do that.

How do your favorite characters travel? Think of Dorothy in *The Wizard of Oz*:

- She travels in a house through a tornado.
- She walks.
- She rides on the backs of winged monkeys.
- She rides in a buggy in Emerald City.

How does Harry travel? We know that Harry walks. But look at the other ways he travels.

- Floo powder
- Invisibility cloaks

- Broomstick
- Riding on a magical creature
- Knight bus
- Portkeys
- An enchanted car
- Hogwarts' express

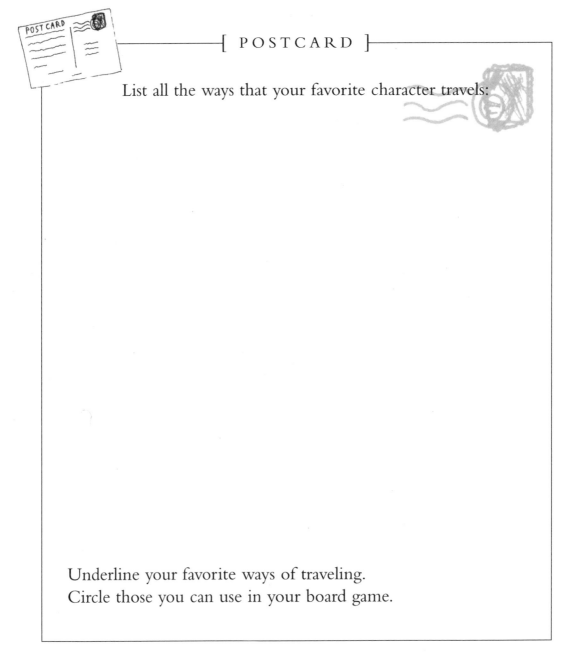

[POSTCARD]

List all the ways that your favorite character travels:

Underline your favorite ways of traveling.
Circle those you can use in your board game.

In the next page, we provide directions on how to make a spinner or dice. You can make a spinner or dice that uses numbers. Dice with numbers or spinners with numbers are what most board games use. Is this what you would like to do? If so, you can skip to p. 54 and learn how to make your own.

But, you might love your favorite book so much you want even to tinker with the dice or spinners. To do this, look at the ways your favorite character travels and make them a part of the dice or spinner. For instance, if your game were based on *The Wizard of Oz* your dice might have these six sides:

- a drawing of a tornado
- winged monkeys
- a buggy
- Dorothy walking alone
- the Scarecrow
- the Wizard sitting on his throne.

In your rules you would explain what happens when you roll the dice. You could say: "Roll the dice. If you roll the tornado, move your game piece ten squares; if you roll the winged monkeys, move your game piece five squares; if you roll the buggy, move your game piece three squares. If you roll Dorothy or the Scarecrow walking, move one square. And if you roll the Wizard, you lose a turn."

In your game, you can match the movement of the dice or the spinner to what happens in the book. You get to use your imagination to match up the movement on the board to the movement in the book. For instance, if yours is a Harry Potter game, your dice might have a picture of Harry walking. This side of the dice would move you forward one space. Another side of the dice might have a picture of an invisibility cloak. This could move you to the other side of the board, while a picture of a broomstick would move you three spaces. Because there are so many ways that Harry travels you can have a lot of fun assigning value to these ways of movement.

To make a dice:

- You can take a block and paint it.
- You can also make a dice from cardboard.
- Two corners of a box, like a cereal box, can be slid together to make a dice.
- Then assign a number or one of the ways your characters travel to each side of the dice.

To make a spinner:

If you prefer to move your players along the board with a spinner, you can design your own spinner. After making the spinner, assign a number or one of the ways your character travels to each section of the spinner.

- Make an arrow.
- Take a round piece of cardboard or the inside of a paper plate.
- Punch a hole in the middle of it.
- Using a pencil and a ruler, divide your circle or "pie" into at least four slices and not more than ten slices.
- If you are using numbers, number each "pie" slice. If you are using methods of travel from your favorite book, draw or write them in the slices. You can go over them later with pen and ink after you have it the way you like it.
- Punch a hole at the end of your arrow.
- Attach the arrow to the cardboard with a brad. Be sure it is not too tight or it will not spin. The smaller the brad, the tighter the spin.

If you decide to use numbers rather than actions from your favorite book, you might choose to use *Roman* numerals (I, II, III, IV, etc.) on your dice or spinner rather than *Arabic* numbers (the regular numbers 1, 2, 3, 4, etc.). Go to the library and find a book about Roman numerals or look at an article in an encyclopedia.

GUIDEPOST

Chance and probability: With this chapter, your child is encountering the issues of chance and probability. Chance is the likelihood that something will happen. When you roll the dice, each number is as likely to come up as any other. You will have six equally likely results. It is this probability, this uncertainty, about the course of events that adds to the excitement of the game. Ask your child what is the likelihood that they might roll a two? The answer is one out of six—1/6.

CHAPTER 11

Tollways and Treasures

If you go on a trip, you may be given some money at the beginning to spend on souvenirs. Usually your spending money is supposed to last until you return home. In your board game, just as you do going on a trip, you and your friends may start off with some money or points, but you also should have the opportunity to get more during the game.

Did you select a goal for your game that involves accumulating money or points? If you did, you need to do three things:

1. Make the rules for the money.
2. Create the money or points.
3. Include stops along the way of your game that involve money or points.

If you are not using money or points as the object to win, you can skip the rest of this chapter.

BEN
SUGGESTS

Make the total number needed to win an even number so that when you have to figure out how many coins or points you need to make for your game, it is easier to divide.

―――――――――――{ POSTCARD }――――――――――――

In your game, how much money or points does someone need to win? _____

Will everyone start off the game with a certain amount of money
or points? _____

If yes, how much _____? (Make this an even number, too.)

Now subtract the amount of money or points that players have at
the beginning from the amount of money or points the players need
to win. Then you will have the number of points players need to get
during the game:

Number to win: _____

Number at beginning: —   _____

Number needed during game: _____

BEN *SUGGESTS*

> I liked what I did, but I realized the goal for the game—
> getting fifty galleons—was set too high. It might take play-
> ing the game to learn this.

How much money or points do you need in all for your game? To
identify how much money you need to make, you have to decide how
many players can play your game at any one time.

BEN *SUGGESTS*

> I had four player pieces that could be used in my game. This
> meant that no more than four people could play the game.
> I would suggest that you not have more than six people
> playing your game at one time. It gets complicated!

How many players do you want to play your game? _____

Each player will have money or points, so you have to make enough to go around. Here is how you can figure out how much money you need in all:

Total number to win: _____

Number of players: x_____

Total number of money or points needed: _____

You now know how much money or points you need. But you still have to decide what *units* your money or points will come in. "Units" means how much each coin or point will be worth. Of course, each coin or point could be worth "1." But if you have to get $1000 to win, you would then need 1000 coins! That would take some time to make!

BEN

SUGGESTS

Here is my super formula for creating money or points. You will want at least two different sizes: like pennies and quarters or dollars and five dollars. On the left side of the page is my example, on the right side is for you to do the math for your game. Imagine that the

Total number of money or points needed for my game is: 200

Total number of money or points needed for your game is: _____

$$2\overline{)100} \quad 50$$

DIVIDE THAT NUMBER IN HALF

$$2\overline{)200} \quad 100$$

$$2\overline{)}$$

I need: 100 coins worth 1 point

You need: _____

_____

$$2\overline{)120} \quad 60$$

This answer shows you how much you need of the smallest unit of money or points.

You now have divided the amount of money or points in half. The number you have is _____. You might decide, like Ben, that two units of money or points is enough. To determine the value of the remaining half of your money or points, divide the total number needed to win by any individual player by 10.

$100 \div 10 = 10$

$120 \div 10 = 12$

In Ben's game, the total needed to win was 50. $50 \div 10 = 5$. So Ben would make 100 coins that were worth 1 point. But clearly he does not need as many coins worth 5 points. How would he figure out how many coins he should make? It's easy: divide the total number needed to win in half. If you need to have 50 points to win, divide 50 in half. The answer is 25. So you would make 25 coins worth 5 points, and 100 coins that were worth 1. Now, it's your turn.

The **total needed to win** in your game is: _____

Now divide that by 10: _____ ÷10 = _____

This is the amount your larger sized coins will be worth in your game.

How many do you need to make?

The total needed to win in your game is: _____

Now divide that by 2: _____ ÷2 = _____

This is how many larger sized coins you need to make.

{ POSTCARD }

This will help you plan how many coins you need to make.

Total number to win the game: _____

Total number you need to have for all the players: _____

The smallest unit value is _____

The total number of the smallest unit value is _____

The largest unit value is _____

The total number of the largest unit value is _____

What we are calling "units" is officially called "denominations" when it refers to money. Go to the library and find out the definition of denominations. Or look under money in the Encyclopedia and find out how other cultures work with currency. (Do you know that word, "currency"? Check it out, too.) This might give you some good ideas in creating your own system.

Sometimes it is easy to get confused when talking about money. If you are confused, ask an adult to help you to figure it out.

On page 57, you figured out that your players need to get_____ amount of money or points to win. How will they get it?

Do you remember the example of Alice in Wonderland needing to get enough money to call home? How would we design the game board with the steps Alice would need to take to reach the goal?

- Alice might start with 10 cents when she falls through the rabbit hole.

+10¢ • She needs to get 75 cents total in order to call home by the end of the game. So she needs to accumulate 65 cents along her journey.

+10¢ • She might pick up 10 cents from the Mad Hatter during the tea party.

−5¢ • She might lose 5 cents when she falls down the hole.

+5 • The White Rabbit might give her 5 cents for getting a pair of gloves.

+20 • The Queen might give her 20 cents for helping her with croquet.

Making Money.

If you are using money or points, here is a way to
   make it.

 Select the material for your money or points. It
might be cardboard, or foil or gold wrapping paper.

 You can paint cardboard with spray paint or cover it
with the foil or wrapping papers.

 Next, find some different sizes of circles around your
houses (coins, bottom of bottles or cans), and trace them
onto your cardboard.

Cut out your shapes.

Or   Trace play money on to construction paper and then
decorate it yourself.

Or   Copy this Gameland money.

Don't worry if you discover you don't have enough. You
can always make more.

61

+10
- The Cheshire cat might help her find 10 cents hidden in his tree.

+10
- The cards might give her 10 cents for helping to paint the roses red.

We still need to figure out how Alice is going to get 15 cents. And we haven't even taken into account that she might not land on all these squares! But part of the fun of a board game is the excitement of the unknown. The most important thing to remember about assigning values to squares is not to make any one square's value so high that the game is easy to win, or so low that the game lasts forever. Our example shows you ways of balancing the value among squares. You can assign value to your squares in the same way, making sure that the players have many chances to gain and lose points. Sound complicated? Don't be worried. It is lots of fun!

If this were going to go on our board, then each one of those actions would go on a sticky note so that we could assign it a square on the board. You need to do the same thing. To get started, imagine that you will have eight squares scattered around the board where you gain money or points and at least three squares scattered around the board

GUIDEPOST

Mathematical Skills: An essential part of most board games is determining how many points things are worth, how many are needed to win, etc. Whether this takes the form of money or points, math skills are needed to determine the guidelines, including addition, subtraction, multiplication, and division. This is probably the hardest part of creating the entire game. It was a challenge for Ben, and it was a challenge for this mom and this librarian to try to unravel the task. Be patient and helpful with your child as they envision a financial or point aspect to their game. Remind them that they can always change it or add to it if they find out that it doesn't work later.

—[POSTCARD]—

How can the players in your game get the amount they need to win in playing the game? The tasks that could be performed by the players and the amount each will be worth will be:

_____ to get/lose _____ points

_____ to get/lose _____ points

_____ to get/lose _____ points

_____ to get/lose _____ points

_____ to get/lose _____ points

_____ to get/lose _____ points

_____ to get/lose _____ points

where you lose money or points. Keeping in mind the total needed to be acquired to win, assign a value to each square. That way you can make sure that, for instance, if you need $1000 you wouldn't cause your players to lose $750 but only ever gain 50 cents!

ASSIGNING VALUE TO YOUR SPACES.

- Look at the spaces you have already created. Are there any that you can assign money or points to if they are landed on? Fill in the sticky notes you have already created with this information.
- For the remaining amount of money or points you are working with, create spaces for them with new sticky notes. Assign the amount of points or money you will get at each space.
- Look at the other ways you may have decided that money or points are going to be gained. Is there anything else you need to do to make sure these ways appear on your board game?

CHAPTER 12

The Hazards of Traveling: Creating Complications

To be exciting, a game has to have challenges. What will prevent you from getting money, or houses, or points? Those are the complications or hazards in the game. Every game, like every story, has to have them. Think, for example, of some of the obstacles Dorothy faces in Oz:

- The witch is trying to get her.
- The poppy field puts her to sleep.
- At first the Cowardly Lion seems frightening.
- A part of the yellow brick road disappears into a crevice.

Or think of some of the obstacles Harry Potter faces:

- His uncle won't let him open a letter addressed to him.
- He gets caught by Filch.
- Ghosts.
- Malfoy and his friends are cruel.
- Snape.
- Howlers.
- Dementors.

- They have to be in classes when they don't want to be.
- Nosy teachers.
- Peeves.
- Mrs. Norris.

You can make these actions and conflicts with people into stops along the board game. These are the things that will make your game exciting. You don't want to get *bored* with your *board* game. You want it to be challenging.

The first way you can create hazards on your board is by making them into spaces.

These spaces might simply be commands:

- Go forward two spaces.
- Go backward two spaces.
- Go back to the beginning.
- Command the player to go to a particular destination.

Then, ask yourself, what exciting things happen at the squares you have already identified. For instance, continuing with the example of *Alice in Wonderland*, you could say,

- You drank the "drink me" bottle. Go back two spaces.
- Fall through the hole. Go to the other side of the board.
- You insult the Queen of Hearts. Lose a turn.

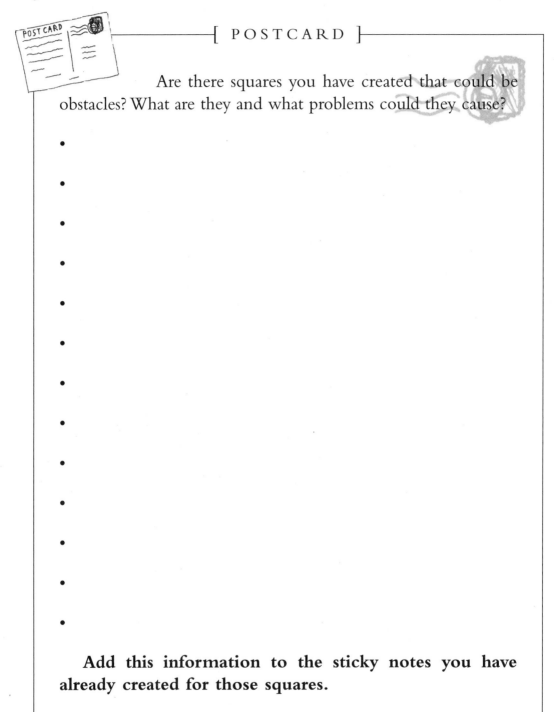

[POSTCARD]

Are there squares you have created that could be obstacles? What are they and what problems could they cause?

-
-
-
-
-
-
-
-
-
-
-
-

Add this information to the sticky notes you have already created for those squares.

Sometimes good things happen at obstacles. Don't forget to include these. For instance, your players might go forward instead of backward or they might get an extra turn instead of losing one.

---[P O S T C A R D]---

   In your favorite book, what **actions occur** or **characters appear** that keep your hero from getting to his or her goal? Look back at your actions postcard on p. 29 for help.

_____

_____

_____

_____

_____

_____

_____

_____

Circle the obstacles that are the most interesting to you.

   You might make the ones that are the most interesting into commands for moving around the board. The other obstacles could be ones that have a point or money value attached to them. For example, an obstacle for Alice could be growing too big to fit in a house or being captured by the Queen. You could decide that the first will result in losing a turn. So you would write "Alice grows too big to fit into house. Lose a turn." The other might be something that causes her to lose money. For being captured by the Queen, she loses X amount. (Your choice.)

Now create new sticky notes for the obstacles you have identified.

BEN SUGGESTS

Magical creatures can be obstacles, too. They can be helpful or they could be hazardous. Even if the reference to them in your book is brief, you could make their role bigger for your board game. For instance, you might say that landing on a griffin means that you move ahead two spaces and that landing on a unicorn means you move backward two spaces. If you land on basilisk you could miss a turn. (Be careful! If you put a griffin and then two spaces later a unicorn, you would simply be caught in an endless circle.)

Are there any magical creatures in your favorite book? Make a list of them:

_____

_____

_____

_____

_____

_____

_____

Go to your local library and find out which ones are mythological creatures that people used to believe existed and which ones your favorite author created using her or his imagination.

See the magical creatures along pages 64-65. You can trace their images and put them on squares of your game if they fit into your story.

Can you make up an imaginary creature? Draw it here:

Make up your own words to describe an imaginary place or creature and include it in your game.

GUIDEPOST

Sequencing: With these exercises your child will develop and use their sequencing skills: learning to put ideas into a logical order. They will also gain an appreciation of the importance of conflict in a story (and game!). These obstacles for the characters introduce excitement into the trip as they play their game as well as inject the element of chance into the outcome.

CHAPTER 13

Double-decker Highway: Taking Your Game to Another Level

Any game can be made more or less challenging according to how many elements it contains. You can take your game to another level! This chapter suggests ways to do that. But you might be very happy with the game you have so far. If so, you can skip to the next chapter.

In order to make your game more challenging, you can add elements to it. Think of the possibilities!:

- You could make trivia or quiz cards with questions on them that your players have to answer.
- You could create additional game boards that your players have to jump to.
- You could make extra items to collect for additional money or points.
- You could take special aspects of your favorite book and have them influence the game.

BEN
SUGGESTS

I made my game more complicated and more fun by including quiz cards with trivia from each Harry Potter book. I also added a space that made a player who landed on it jump to a Quidditch game board and play a game of Quidditch before being allowed back on to the regular board. You can add something to confuse the regular play or free you from a task. I added broomsticks, letters, and Knight bus tokens to do this. For instance, the Knight bus tokens excused you from a penalty or direction that you didn't want to follow.

POSTCARD

—{ POSTCARD }—

What items do you think of when you think of the magical world created in your favorite book?

Draw pictures of those or write down words you think of:

Can they become a part of your game?

CREATING QUIZ CARDS

Sometimes when you love a book, you read it again and again. And in reading it more than once you begin to remember lots of details about what happens and facts about the characters and what they like. That's what happened with Ben and Harry Potter. You feel like you know the book from the inside out. What better way to make your game more exciting or give your game more depth than to challenge your players about their knowledge of the book? You can create quiz cards that ask questions about details in the book. For instance, you might ask, "What did Alice grab when she was falling down the rabbit hole?

BEN

SUGGESTS

It was fun to think of the questions. I thought of some of the easiest things that I knew about the books and some of the hardest things: Like how many Sickles in a Galleon, and how many Knuts are in five Galleons. I would look back at the books, to get some ideas and to make sure the answers were correct. I decided that the challenging questions would pay more money than the easier ones if you got them right. So, for each question I put how many Galleons you would get. I printed them out from the computer on labels. Then I glued them onto three-by-five index cards.

Facts that you know about your favorite book can become the answers to your quiz card questions. What do you need to ask? For instance, if the fact is "Gryffindor colors are red and gold" you could ask, "What colors are associated with Gryffindor?"

If you create quiz cards, be precise and accurate in asking your questions. If you are not sure, look it up in the book. You don't want to have the wrong information. After you have brainstormed questions and answers, you will begin to see how much fun it is to ask questions about your book. When you have at least ten questions you can begin to make your cards. Don't forget to use your journal or three-by-five cards

[POSTCARD]

Brainstorm facts about important and unimportant things that happen in your book:

1. _____

2. _____

3. _____

4. _____

5. _____

6. _____

7. _____

8. _____

9. _____

10. _____

11. _____

12. _____

13. _____

14. _____

15. _____

16. _____

17. _____

18. _____

19. _____

20. _____

whenever you have a good idea for a quiz card. For as long as you are playing this game, you will probably want to continue to create quiz cards to keep the game exciting, and because asking questions like these is fun! (Not to mention that you don't want your friends to know all the answers after they have played it a few times!)

Once you have identified the possible questions and answers, you need to decide what will happen to your players if they answer correctly and what will happen to them if they cannot answer the question.

- Do they gain or lose points or money?
- Do they move forward or backward depending on how they answer?
- Do they lose or gain a turn?

Include this information on each quiz card, so the player, after answering, will know what they have to do.

If you want to make your quiz cards complicated, you can give points or money for answering the quiz cards correctly depending on how hard they are. For instance, what you consider an easy question would receive one point and a really hard question might get five points. Note the amount of the award on each card, so there is no confusion.

BEN

SUGGESTS

I realized that my quiz cards could be color coded. If the book you love has sequels, like *Alice in Wonderland, The Wizard of Oz*, or the Harry Potter series, you can color code the quiz cards to each book. Say you are basing your quiz card questions on the first three Oz books. You might color code them so that questions for *The Wonderful Wizard of Oz* are red; questions for the second book in this series, *The Land of Oz,* might be green; and questions for *Ozma of Oz*, the third book in that series, might be blue. If you are playing with someone who has only read the first book in the series you would only use red cards. If you are playing with someone who has read the first two books, you would play with red and green cards. And if *all* of you have read all three books, then you can use all the quiz cards you have.

Making your quiz cards

- Organize your questions and answers.
- Take your index cards.
- Put one question on each card. Write the answer on the other side upside down.
- Indicate what happens with a right or wrong answer: How much money/points does one earn or lose? Do you have to move forward or backward depending on if you get the answer right or wrong?

Once you have decided what extra challenges you wish to add to your game, you need to create spaces on your board for these elements.

{ POSTCARD }

What have you decided to add?

- _____
- _____
- _____
- _____
- _____
- _____
- _____

Create a sticky note for each space that you need to add. For instance, if you are adding quiz cards, you might decide that you want two spaces for quiz cards to be drawn. Then you would create two sticky notes and find two spaces on the board to fit them. Be sure that the space is clear in its instruction. For instance, the space could read, "Draw a quiz card" or "go to other board."

DETOUR

Did you ever wonder how your author came up with such creative ideas? Go to the library and find out about your author. Look in the set of reference books called *Something about the Author.* Your public library will probably have it, and, if they do, it will always be there because you have to read this reference book in the library—you can't take it out. You might also see if the library has a biography about your author. What is the most interesting thing you learned about your author?

GUIDEPOST

GUIDEPOST

Synthesis: As they glean trivia-type information and put it in the form of questions, your child will gain an even more in-depth comprehension of the book, and will develop a greater appreciation for the author's techniques. They will develop a greater love for the author's imaginative use of language and tiny details that make the reading of the book a richer experience. In addition, quiz cards address the competitive spirit of children who like to know the right answers. Even our popular culture is consumed with trivia as shown by the current successful television game shows that use trivia as the basis for winning or losing. If your child wants to pursue creating extra elements, aid them by asking thought-provoking questions about elements in their book that they enjoyed, i.e., "Why do you think the Mad Hatter's tea party lasted so long?" "Could you make your players stop and have tea before they go on?" Or you could help them with trivia questions about *Alice in Wonderland.* Often these sorts of questions become apparent when you are reading aloud to your child. Even if you have shared the joy of this book already together, take the time to savor it yet again, and you will be amazed at how many ideas for quiz questions will arise as your child listens to this book or a favorite part of it being read out loud.

CHAPTER 14

Sightseeing: Finishing Your Board

Now is the time to put your board all together! It is thrilling to watch your board take final shape. There are several enjoyable steps. You have to finish your spaces, decorate your board, and name your game.

At this point, you should have created as many sticky notes for your game as there are spaces on your game board. If you haven't filled all your spaces, you can add spaces such as "walk in the woods" or "stop for a rest." It is up to you whether you want something to happen on these spaces or not. If you do, have fun—tell them they can go forwards or backwards, or gain a turn or lose a turn. Or they can land on it and have nothing to do—it's up to you! Make sticky notes for these additional spaces. Is your board now filled?

Now you can transfer what you have written on the sticky notes to each space you have created on your game board! Print clearly so that your players can read the spaces. You might write in pencil first to make sure everything is where you want it, and then later go over it with a marker or pen.

After your game spaces are filled in, what about the empty space around it and in the middle? Decorating your board gives you a chance to include more details from your book. What is the setting of your favorite book? *Where* does everything happen in your game? In the forest? In an ocean? In a house or a museum? Does it take place outside in a garden or a maze? Down a rabbit hole? In a castle? In a school for wizards? In a fantasy land?

Now you can make the *where* of your favorite book come alive by adding details to your board game. How do you decide what to add? This postcard will help you.

{ POSTCARD }

The favorite part of my book takes place in _____

Describe this place: _____

_____

_____

What colors are in it? _____

_____

What living creatures are in it? _____

Is it a small place or a large place? _____

How does the author describe this place? _____

_____

_____

Look at your answers. Circle anything that you can include in your board game. For instance, you might have said that red and green are the colors. Then you could paint your board red and green. Or you might have said it takes place in a forest. You can draw trees or paste leaves onto your board.

Your possibilities are limitless. So how do you decide what to add?

BEN
SUGGESTS

Begin with what you already have around the house. Part of my game took place in a forest, so I used some lichen from a hobby shop to make trees. I also used rocks, old game pieces, colored foil, and spray paint.* See what your local hardware store has as samples that you might get for free. Use pieces and parts of old games and toys you have around the house. I also used lots of things we had gotten at garage sales. Perhaps you can go with an adult to some garage or yard sales or flea markets. What kind of things can you buy at a garage sale or a flea market? Everything! I often got replacement parts for my favorite game, Monopoly™!

* To learn how Ben decorated his boards, the details that he put on them, and the way he made them three-dimensional, read his companion book, *My Year with Harry Potter*.

Ben's tips for going to a garage sale or a flea market:

If there is something that you want, hold on to it. Don't leave it on the table or wherever it is, because it might be gone by the time you truly decide. Pick it up and carry it with you.

Be suspicious of places without price tags. They are sizing up their buyers.

Don't look like you really, really want it. Because they'll raise the price or be less likely to bargain.

If you do bargain, sometimes what you should do is offer half of what they are asking. Say they are asking $5.00 and you offer $2.50, they might respond, "Well, the least I'll do is $3.50."

Try to get going before 10:00 a.m. Some of the best things might be gone if you wait too long.

Rule of thumb: They say you should only pay one-fifth of what the thing is worth when it is new.

Ask about things, but don't assume anything electrical works works—*even* if you are told that it does.

NAMING YOUR GAME

What about a name? Have you already been calling your board game by a name? If not, what do you want to call your game? Look at your game board. How does it look now that the spaces are filled in and it is decorated? Does a name leap to mind as you look at it?

{ POSTCARD }

Brainstorm some titles for your game:

1. _____

2. _____

3. _____

4. _____

5. _____

Circle the one you like the best.

CHAPTER 15

Consulting the Guidebook: Writing Down Your Rules

R ules, like good stories, tell us who, what, when, how, and why. In the last chapter, you completed the *where*. You now have your own beautiful and unique board. But what is going to happen and why? Your rules will tell you.

BEN SUGGESTS

I had so many parts to my game and so many ideas for my game, that when I went to write down my rules it was both fun and challenging. I worked with my mother at a computer so that I could constantly check the list of items I wanted to include and move the text of the rules around. Because someone was helping me, it was easier to explain the rules. You might want to have someone work with you on this part—a friend, a relative, a teacher. Things that I thought were obvious I realized I had to explain to someone who had never seen my game before. And that's how I learned how important rules are. I also learned that in writing these down I was nearly done!

You might want to look at the rules for your favorite board game to give you ideas about just how rules work. Perhaps now that you have created your own game, these rules will no longer be just some boring piece of paper. They aren't. They are the way that inventors share their games. And you, because you know the rules, can bring the game to life.

The rules will be influenced by how many parts you have put into your game and when those parts will be used.

How do you write your rules?

─┤ P O S T C A R D ├─

List all the items in your game. This means the game pieces, the coins, the spinner, or dice, any extras (like quiz cards) that you have added:

- _____
- _____
- _____
- _____
- _____
- _____
- _____
- _____

If you have more items than this space allows, continue making your list on a piece of a paper or in your journal. Using this list as a checklist, describe

1. What each item is.

2. When it is used.

3. What each item does.

(Continued on next page)

(Continued from previous page)

For instance, you might have listed: spinners, points, and owls. You would write:

Players will move by spinning the spinner. (If you designed your own spinner according to the instructions on p. 54, now is the time to explain how your spinner works. Did you create images instead of using numbers? Tell the players what they will do when they land on each image.)

They will gain points by _____.
(Here you would list how points are gained in your game.)

When you land on a space that says "an owl lands" you receive an owl. (Then you would describe what the owl offers in the game.)

Continue in this way, describing each element of your game. If you can use a computer for this part, it is easier, because like Ben you might need to move items in your rules around to make them clearer.

Now look at your rules. Do your rules tell your players *who*, *what*, *how*, and *when*? Use this rules checklist to help you.

__ Do your rules tell *what* is the object of the game?

__ Do your rules tell *who* plays the game?

__ Do your rules tell *how* many people play the game?

__ Do your rules tell *who* goes first?

__ Do your rules tell *what* your players start with? Do they start with points or money or something else and how much?

__ Do your rules tell *how* you get started? (roll dice? Spin spinner?)

__ Do your rules tell *how* they move around the board?

__ Do your rules tell *when* is it over?

__ Do your rules tell *how* you know who wins?

__ Do your rules explain *when* all the extra things are used and *what* they do? (quiz cards, extra boards, etc.?)

(Continued on next page)

[POSTCARD]

(Continued from previous page)

After you have checked to make sure your rules contain all of this information, look at your rules one more time. The best rules are simple and clear and go in order of how the game is played. Do you need to re-order your rules so that they go in order? Will others be able to read your rules? Are they too long—or too short? Take your final copy of your rules and put it with your game so that all players can read them if they need to, or if a question arises about something in the game.

Find a book about games in your library. Look at all the interesting names they have. Which names of games make you want to read more about the game and learn how to play them? Read the instructions for some of these games. Are they easy to understand? Which game sounds the most fun?

GUIDEPOST

Communication: When your child sits down to write the rules of the game, they may need your help. Be patient. Ask questions. Listen to their answers and help your child think through how all the parts of their game come together. Your child will be making use of essential communication skills—using clear, step-by-step language to convey meaning to another person. They will find themselves making use of classic outlining skills, exhibiting understanding of a main idea or starting point, and a conclusion or ending point. This takes time. Don't let them feel discouraged. It's okay to do this in several stages and not in one sitting.

CHAPTER 16

Welcome to Gameland

You have made the board and written the rules. You know how you are going to move around the board and what it takes to win.

Now you get to play your game with other players!

You might want to start with just one other player. Someone who will be patient as you discover any bumps in the road of your game. Explain your game slowly. Remember this is a new game to them. Listen carefully to their questions as you play. Are they asking things that should be added to your rules? Do their questions let you know that your rules need to be written more clearly? Or has a problem occurred? Is there something you want to rethink or change?

BEN

SUGGESTS

Before I played my game with friends, I played it with my mom. We checked the rules as we went to make sure that I had everything clear in the rules. We noticed that it took a long time to get any money in my game and we never actually finished it. So I had to think about how money worked in my game.

You are trying out your game to see if it works. This is like test driving a car or performing an experiment. Take notes if you discover something that just doesn't work so that you can fix the problem later.

{ P O S T C A R D }

How did the game work? _____

_____

_____

What worked the best? _____

_____

What didn't work? _____

_____

Would you like to take something out? _____

_____

_____

Would you like to add something? _____

_____

_____

If you have decided to make changes, now is the time to do so. After you have made the changes and updated your rules, play your game again with the same person or add another person. Is the game working better now?

Aren't you proud of yourself for inventing your own game? Would you like to learn about other children who have invented something wonderful? Go to your library and see if they have any of these books:

- Arlene Erlbach, *The Kids' Invention Book*. Minneapolis: Lerner Publications Co, 1997.
- Frances A. Karnes, *Girls and Young Women Inventing: 20 True Stories about Inventors and their Inventions*. Minneapolis: Free Spirit Publisher, 1995.
- Catherine Thimmesh, *Girls Think of Everything: Stories of Ingenious Inventions by Women*. Boston: Houghton Mifflin, 2000.
- Tom Tucker, *Brainstorm!: The Stories of Twenty American Kid Inventors*. New York: Farrar, Straus and Giroux, 1995.
- Don L. Wulffson, *The Kid Who Invented the Popsicle and Other Surprising Stories about Inventions*. New York: Cobblehill Books, 1997.

GUIDEPOST

Evaluation and Celebration: Assessing one's product or performance is an important life skill. After all, evaluating our own efforts helps us grow and reflect on our own abilities and interests. Help your child understand the importance of realizing that their game can still be worked on, that it might not be perfect at first. It's okay to admit that something doesn't work and then try to make it better. Now is also the time to celebrate completing the game by filling out the certificate found at the end of the book. There are four blanks to fill in. The first, "Presented to," of course is the one for your child's name. The second, "in journeying to," is the place where you fill in the name of their favorite book. The third blank space, "by creating," is for the name of their game. Finally, ask them to identify their favorite character and sign the certificate with that character's name.

You can also help your child throw a party so they can enjoy their achievement with friends. Part of evaluation is celebration. Let your child celebrate and share their creativity! See the next chapter for some suggestions.

CHAPTER 17

Home Again:
How to Have a "Make Your
Own Board Game" Party

You have had so much fun making your own game that maybe you would like to share your excitement with your friends. Or, you want to help your friends to help make their own game. A "Make Your Own Board Game" party can be lots of fun! Our local library had one and the kids had a great time.

What will you need?

Definitely, you'll need your parents help. Work with them to pick a time that is good for them and good for you.

Think about the kind of game you want your friends to design and the time that will be available. One hour? There is a lot you can do in an hour! Do you want to design a game as a pattern your friends could use? Of course, encouraging your friends to be creative and invent their own game will be part of the fun.

You should probably decide whether you want the basic game to use spinners or dice, and have those traced for your friends already.

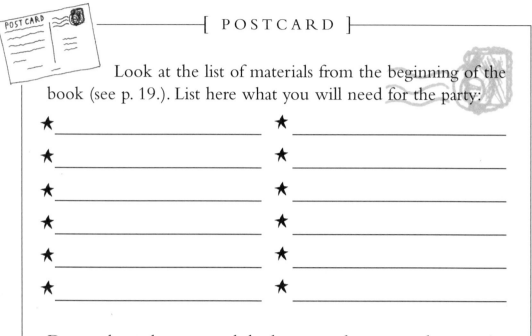

{ POSTCARD }

Look at the list of materials from the beginning of the book (see p. 19.). List here what you will need for the party:

★ _____   ★ _____

★ _____   ★ _____

★ _____   ★ _____

★ _____   ★ _____

★ _____   ★ _____

★ _____   ★ _____

Do you have these around the house or do you need to acquire them? Show your list to your parents if you don't have these items around the house and ask for their help.

Create your own invitation! Perhaps you will make it look like a board game and put the information in the squares of the game. It might look something like this: Add your own drawings and fill in the blanks. If you know what book you want to base the party and board game on—tell your friends in the invitation.

Or use the Origami owl on page 49 as an invitation. Kids would have to unfold their owl to read the invitation. Or create your own invitation!

PARTY THEMES

1. Design your own game. Each child designs his or her own game, alone or in groups, and then exchanges the game and plays each other's game.
2. A game marathon. Make several copies of your game, and let your friends try it out. Give prizes to the winners.
3. Base your party on your book instead. Have an "Oz" or "Potter" party.

PARTY ACTIVITIES

*   You can look back through this book at things you have made, and pick some of your favorite activities to share with your friends.
*   You can decorate wooden dowel sticks with streamers, ribbons, feathers, etc. for a festive, magical feeling.
*   Make your own broomstick: get straw, dowel sticks, and rope, and each child can make their own broomstick.
*   Face painting—each child can have their face painted as a favorite character.
*   Pin the wings on the dragon. You can copy the dragon on the next pages. Make lots of copies of the wings and let your friends color them. Then, you and your friends can try to pin the wings on.

When the party is over, the objects that your friends have made can be their party favors.

What sort of refreshments would you serve at your party?

Let your favorite book help you decide. Is *The Wizard of Oz* your favorite book? Serve green food! What about *Alice in Wonderland*? Have a tea party and serve "Eat Me" cupcakes and "Drink Me" punch. (The punch could be your favorite juice with sparkling water.)

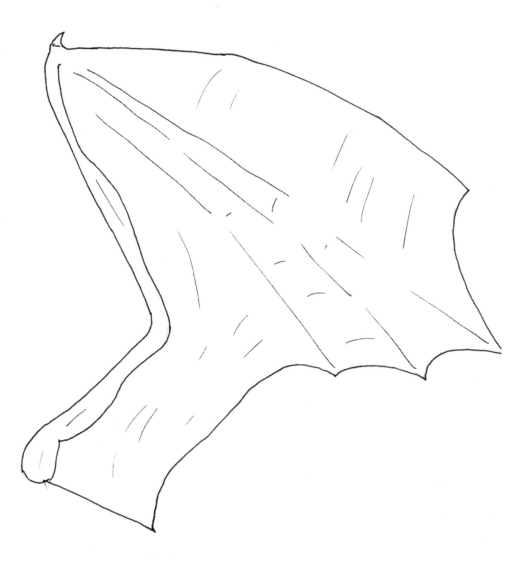

Go to your library and look at books with ideas for parties, crafts, decorations, as well as cookbooks for kids. If your book is set in another country, ask your librarian to help find cookbooks with recipes from other countries or, if the book is historical fiction, ask your librarian to help you find historical cookbooks. Or find out about tea!

How do the British have tea? When is it? Why is it important? When did they start making it a part of their culture? What food is served with the tea? What is a scone? Have you ever had marmalade?

BEN

SUGGESTS

If the Harry Potter series is your favorite, here are some ideas:

- Get jelly beans and have a contest to name the flavors.
- Get some lollipops that are really, really hot, and print out labels that say "Acid Pops."
- Get an ice mold for a mouse and pour apple juice in it, add different types of fruit, freeze, unmold, and put them on a tray and call them "ice mice."
- Get Sparkly Apple Cider and, using food coloring, color it to look orange. Serve it as "Pumpkin Juice." Put it in a kettle to look like a cauldron or, if it's wintertime, serve a favorite drink like hot chocolate.

There is nothing as great as a good book that you can love over and over again. EXCEPT… sharing a good book with your best friends. And once you are "home again"—once you have had your party and played your game and shared the fun and creativity with your friends, guess what? You can do it all again. Maybe you have another favorite book. Do you? Just think, when you are ready, you can make the Journey to Gameland again.

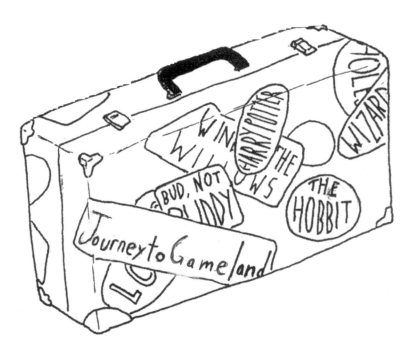

Finding Platform 9¾, the Rabbit Hole, or the Yellow Brick Road: Hints for Getting Started

N eed help getting started? Here's our librarian's list of great children's books and some ideas for games based upon them. Go to your local library for more suggestions of great books to read by yourself or with your family. If we list a book without any publishing information, that means there are several editions of that book available. Thumb through the different editions and pick the one you like the best.

Harry Potter and the Chamber of Secrets by J. K. Rowling. New York: Arthur A. Levine, 1999.

Harry Potter and the Goblet of Fire by J. K. Rowling. New York: Arthur A. Levine, 2000.

Harry Potter and the Prizoner of Azkaban by J. K. Rowling. New York: Arthur A. Levine, 1999.

Harry Potter and the Sorcerer's Stone by J. K. Rowling. New York: Arthur A. Levine, 1999.

Ben had lots of fun making a board game from these books (he made his game before Harry Potter and the Goblet of Fire *was published).*

You can read about how he did it in his book, My Year With Harry Potter. *Maybe you've already begun to think about how you can make your own board game....*

Charlotte's Web by E. B. White. New York: HarperCollins, 1973.
Help Wilbur and his friends get across the farmyard from house to barn to visit Charlotte.

The Secret Garden by Frances Hodgson Burnett.
Help Mary Lennox and her friends find her secret garden and identify different plants they find there.

Alice's Adventures in Wonderland by Lewis Carroll.
Can Alice and the March Hare make it to the Mad Hatter's tea party in time?

The Mouse and the Motorcycle by Beverly Cleary. New York: Morrow, 1965.
Help Ralph make it safely through Mountain View Inn to Keith's room. (You could have different colored mice as playing pieces.)

Pinocchio by Carlo Collodi
Can Pinocchio make it back home to Geppetto's shop?

Help Pinocchio become a real boy by getting through three obstacles. (Pick your favorites from the book.)

The Hobbit by J. R. R Tolkien
You and Bilbo must get to the Lonely Mountain to find Smaug's treasure.

Holes by Louis Sachar. New York: Farrar, Straus, and Giroux, 1998.
Stanley Yelnats must escape from Camp Green Lake and find the buried treasure. Who will be the first player to find it?

From the Mixed-Up Files of Mrs. Basil E. Frankweiler by E. L. Konigsburg. New York: Atheneum, 1967.
Claudia and Jamie and you need to find the mysterious statue inside the Metropolitan Museum of Art.

My Side of the Mountain by Jean Craighead George. New York:
Dutton, 1988.
Help Sam Gribley find all he needs to survive in the Catskill Mountains.

Hatchet by Gary Paulsen. New York: Simon & Schuster, 1987.
Be like Brian and find your way to shelter in the wilderness.

The Wonderful Wizard of Oz by Frank L. Baum.
The characters must get from Munchkin Land to Emerald City.

Little House on the Prairie by Laura Ingalls Wilder. New York: Harper-
Collins, 1953.
Help the Wilder family travel to their new home.

Peter Pan by J.M. Barrie.
Wendy must get from London to NeverNever Land. How will she?

Peter must get from his camp to Captain Hook's lair. How will he?

Find a way to get from Hook's ship to the Lost Boys' camp.

Charlie and the Chocolate Factory by Roald Dahl. New York: Penguin,
1988.
*The players, like Charlie, need to get a golden ticket and go through the
factory to win Mr. Wonka's greatest prize.*

The Wind in the Willows by Kenneth Grahame.
*Mole and the other players need to make it through Wild Wood to find
Badger.*

Half Magic by Edward Eager. New York: Harcourt, 1999.
*Mark, Katharine, Martha, and Jane need to find the magic coin so they
can make double wishes. Which player gets to the magic coin first?*

My Father's Dragon by Ruth Stiles Gannett. New York: Random
House, 1948.
*Elmer Elevator and the other players need to go from the Island of
Tangerina to Wild Island to find the dragon, while collecting a tangerine,
bubble gum, and another item of your choice.*

The Phantom Tollbooth by Norton Juster. New York: Random House, 1989.
   Milo and the other players need to get from Dictionopolis through the Land of Expectations and the Castle in the Air back to his magical tollbooth to get home. Make quiz cards based on your favorite words in the book.

The Jungle Book by Rudyard Kipling.
   You and Mowgli must get through the jungle to the wolf cave, avoiding the dreaded Shere Khan and other jungle hazards.

A Wrinkle in Time by Madeleine L'Engle. New York: Dell, 1976.
   Follow Meg, Calvin, and Charles Wallace through multi-dimensional worlds in search of Meg's father. Make a three-dimensional board!

The Lion, the Witch, and the Wardrobe by C. S. Lewis. New York: HarperCollins, 1997.
   The children need to find their way from the castle of Cair Paravel in Narnia to the magical wardrobe. What wonderful creatures can help you?

Winnie–the–Pooh by A. A. Milne. New York: Dutton, 1961.
   Pooh needs to get through the 100 Acre Wood to see Christopher Robin (look at the map at the front of the book for ideas). Everyone could have a different little bear as a playing piece.

Bud, Not Buddy by Christopher Paul Curtis. New York: Delacorte, 1999.
   Help Bud take his road trip to find his father. Don't forget your suitcase. Use rocks, like those Bud loved as game pieces!

The Stories Julian Tells by Ann Cameron. New York: Pantheon, 1981.
   Help Julian to get through his day, helping him to avoid getting into trouble and finding his friends while telling great stories. Different squares could require a story from the player.

The *Junie B. Jones* series by Barbara Park. New York: Random House, 1992.
   Junie B. Jones needs to get from the school bus to her classroom without getting into trouble. Which of you will make it to the classroom before the bell rings?

For younger readers, simple games from fairy tales such as:

★ *Goldilocks and the Three Bears*
> *The board could be a diagram of a house. Each player has to do something in each room.*

★ *Little Red Riding Hood*
> *Get to Grandma's safely.*

★ *Hansel and Gretel*
> *Get from witch's cottage back to father.*

★ *Three Little Pigs*
> *Find the brick house and be safe from the wolf.*

★ *The Frog Prince*
> *Go from lily pad to castle to get kissed.*

★ *Princess and the Pea*
> *Find the pea and get a crown!*

APPENDIX B

Books for Parents, Teachers, and Librarians

Bauermeister, Erica. *Let's Hear it for the Girls: 375 Great Books for Readers 2–14*. New York: Penguin, 1997.

Carter, Betty. *Best Books for Young Adults*. Chicago: American Library Association, 2000.

Freeman, Judy. *More Books Kids Will Sit Still For: A Read-Aloud Guide*. New Providence, NJ: R. R. Bowker, 1995.

Gillespie, John T., ed. *Best Books for Children: Preschool through Grade 6*. New Providence, NJ: R. R. Bowker, 1998.

Helbig, Alethea. *Many Peoples, One Land: A Guide to New Multicultural Literature for Children and Young Adults*. Westport, CT: Greenwood Press, 2001.

Lynn, Ruth Nadelman. *Fantasy Literature for Children and Young Adults: An Annotated Bibliography*. New Providence, NJ: R. R. Bowker, 1995.

Muse, Daphne, ed. *The New Press Guide to Multicultural Resources for Young Readers*. New York: Free Press, 1997.

Odean, Kathleen. *Great Books for Boys: More than 600 Books for Boys 2 to 14*. New York: Ballantine Books, 1998.

Odean, Kathleen. *Great Books for Girls: Over 600 Books to Inspire Today's Girls and Tomorrow's Women*. New York: Ballantine Books, 1997.

Rand, Donna. *Black Books Galore!: Guide to Great African-American Children's Books*. New York: Wiley, 1998.

Spencer, Pam. *What Do Young Adults Read Next?: A Reader's Guide to Fiction for Young Adults*. Detroit: Gale Group, 1999.

Spencer, Pam. *What Do Children Read Next?: A Reader's Guide to Fiction for Children*. Detroit: Gale Research, 1994.

Toussaint, Pamela. *Great Books for African-American Children*. New York: Plume, 1999.

Trelease, Jim. *The Read-Aloud Handbook*. New York: Penguin Books, 1995.

ACKNOWLEDGMENTS

We thank the Richardson Public Library for its support and willingness to sponsor a "Make Your Own Harry Potter Game" program. The program was the catalyst for this book. In this day and age of electronics, we wish to celebrate the value that public libraries still have for children and their families.

Ben wants to thank his teachers at Hamilton Park Pacesetter Magnet Elementary School and the Richardson Independent School District for providing the impetus for his game through sponsoring the Invention Convention. He especially thanks his gifted teachers, Ms. Gavigan, Ms. Villanueva, Ms. Patel, Mr. Dodd, Ms. Molotsky, and Ms. Dowell.

We thank Douglas Buchanan for entering into the spirit of the book with his illustrations and suggestions. Gene Gollogly for believing in this book, Stefan Killen for designing it, and Martin Rowe for entering into the spirit of this book while shepherding it through the publication process.

The authors wish to acknowledge the joyful cooperation of working together. The adult authors wish to acknowledge Ben's patience in explaining how he made his own game to us. We would also like to acknowledge each other's creativity and the role that each of us had in putting this book together. It took three of us!

We are grateful for the influence and inspiration of J. K. Rowling's books as well as other beloved authors of books both past and present. We'll spare you *our* list of favorite books!

One more letter. A letter to Ben!

Here's your chance to write to Ben and tell him if you created your own game. He'll read your comments, and we'll also use them to make a better book!

Your name _____

Your address _____

_____

Your age _____

Did you like *Journey to Gameland?* _____

Why? _____

_____

_____

What book did you use to make your own game? _____

What ideas did you like the best? _____

_____

_____

What ideas didn't work for you? _____

_____

How could this book be better? _____

_____

Is there anything else you want to tell Ben? _____

_____

When you have told Ben what you want to tell him, cut out this page, fold it, tape it, put a stamp on it and mail it to Ben. His address is printed on the other side of this page. You can also email him at ben@mybookgames.com.

From:

_____

_____

_____

To: Ben Buchanan
     Lantern Books/Booklight, Inc.
     1 Union Square West, Suite 201
     New York, New York 10003

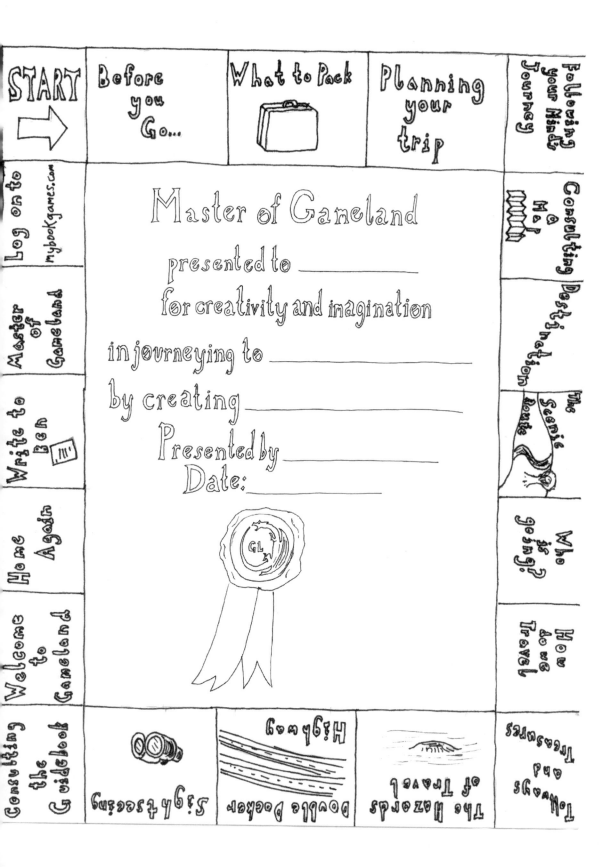

START →

Before you Go...

What to Pack

Planning your trip

Following your Mind's Journey

Log on to mybookgames.com

Master of Gameland

Write to Ben

Home to Again

Welcome to Gameland

Consulting the Guidebook

Sightseeing

Double Decker Highway

The Hazards of Travel

Tollways and Treasures

How do we Travel

Who is going?

The Scenic

Consulting Destination Route

Mail

Master of Gameland

presented to _____

for creativity and imagination

in journeying to _____

by creating _____

Presented by _____

Date: _____

GL